# Red Panda

Learn About Red Pandas-Amazing Pictures & Fun Facts

Spencer Jones

# Disclaimer

# The Life of the Red Panda

The red panda is a small tree animal that is native to the southwestern part of China and the eastern Himalayas. These animals are secretive and shy, making them hard to observe. They are protected animals because their population is decreasing and hunting them is illegal. The countries of Nepal, China, India, Bhutan and even Burma have protected areas for the red pandas.

# How Red Pandas Are Grouped

The red panda is considered to be a vulnerable animal because there are only about 10,000 mature examples of its population living around the world. They are subdivided into two:

1. Styan's Red Panda – they live in parts of northern Burma and southern China.

2. Western Red Panda – can be found in Bhutan, Assam, Nepal, and Sikkim.

Their main differences are their skull size, teeth and skin color.

Relatives of the Red Panda

The red panda is thought to be a relative of the raccoons because their physical features are similar. But by knowing their eating skills and fossil records, we can ascertain that they are from a separate family. A red panda is not considered a bear, not related to the giant panda, and is not a raccoon either. It is a member of the Musteloids, a family of animals which includes weasels, otters, badgers and martens.

# Meet the Red Panda's Cousins

The red panda is thought to be a relative of the raccoons because their physical features are similar. But by knowing their eating skills and fossil records, we can ascertain that they are from a separate family. A red panda is not considered a bear, not related to the giant panda, and is not a raccoon either. It is a member of the Musteloids, a family of animals which includes weasels, otters, badgers and martens.

# How the Red Panda Looks Like

Also called the red cat-bear and lesser panda, this animal's typical size and growth is the same as that of a house cat. They have a black-colored belly and limbs, with white markings at the sides of their head. Their big bushy tail may give them an additional length of 18 inches and they use it for balance and as a wraparound coat during cold weather. Their head is rounded, their eyes are brownish red in color and their noses are black.

# Where They Live

The Himalayan forests, where the weather changes are mild, are considered to be habitats of the red panda along with the forests at the foothills of western Nepal. They spend most of their time living in the trees and they sleep in high places. As the forests in their habitat are thinning, red pandas are becoming endangered. Their habitat becomes smaller as more forests are being destroyed due to logging.

# How Red Pandas Clean and Groom Themselves

The red pandas clean themselves just like cats do. They lick and stretch their body and they wash their face using their front and hind paws. They do their grooming while sitting on tree branches. They lick through their chests, legs, tails, and other parts of their body including their tail which they draw up to their face using their front paws.

# What a Typical Red Panda Meal Consists of

The red pandas are omnivorous animals and they forage in the trees. Bamboo makes up about two thirds of their diet - they consume about 1.5 kilograms of fresh bamboo leaves and 4 kilograms of fresh bamboo shoots daily. Their meals may also include small birds, eggs, insects, and other small mammals. They also eat flowers and berries, roots, mushrooms, acorns, lichens and grasses.

Because of their low calorie diet, they tend to just eat and sleep throughout their lives. To help protect the red pandas all over the world, different organizations have started working with the Red Panda Management Group in North America, India, Japan, Australia and China to continue various captive-breeding programs. These programs involve captive red pandas which are taken care of in zoos and specialty places to help produce more red pandas.

# The Red Panda's Social Life

The red panda mainly lives on its own and is a territorial creature. They only get along with other red pandas during the mating season. Most of the time, they are quiet but they make tweeting or whistling noises to communicate with other red pandas. This nocturnal animal sleeps on branches or in tree hollows during the day and becomes more active in the late afternoon until the early hours of the evening.

# Life in Captivity

The red panda can easily adapt to a life in captivity, making it a common animal attraction in different zoos all over the world. There have been more than 300 red pandas born in captivity since 1992 and more than 300 red pandas are known to live in 85 different institutions worldwide. The largest number of captive red panda births is in Knoxville Zoo, with 101 born as of 2011.

# How Cute Baby Red Pandas Are Made

The red panda only mingles with other red pandas in the wild for mating. It may mate with more than one partner during their mating season which occurs in the middle of January up to early March. Before a female red panda gives birth, it starts collecting materials for its nest, which may include grass, leaves and brushwood. The nest is then built in a hollow tree or a rock crevice.

# The Cute Little Baby Pandas

After carrying the babies in their womb for about 112 to 158 days, the female red panda then gives birth to between one and four deaf and blind cubs. Each cub weighs about 110 to 130 grams and gets cleaned by the mother. After the first week of birth, the mother starts to spend most of her time outside the nest, checking every few hours to groom and nurse the babies. The red panda cubs start to open their eyes at around the third week and within 3 months; they have already matured physically and start to leave their nest to look for food on their own.

# Red Pandas in Cultures and Traditions

The red panda was considered as the state animal of Sikkim, India, and was even considered as the mascot for the Darjeeling Tea Festival in the early 1990s. A red panda named Futa became a popular tourist attraction in Japan because of its ability to stand upright for about 10 seconds at a time. The red panda, which is also commonly known as "firefox" is also being related to the icon of a popular web browser called Firefox, but the logo does not really depict the red panda's image.

# Natural Enemies of Red Pandas

The red panda is considered as prey by snow leopards, wild dogs, humans and even martens, which are members of the same family of the red panda. They try to escape any threat or danger by climbing up a tree or a rock column. They stand upright using their hind legs and stretch up their arms to make them appear larger. They then use the claws of their front paws to defend themselves against predators.

# Conservation of Red Pandas

With continuous tree logging and hunting of the red panda in the wild, they are starting to become threatened creatures. Conservation efforts in different countries include a total ban of red panda hunting and also the provision of protected areas of habitat. In eastern Nepal's Ilam District, a community cares for a forest that serves as home for 15 red pandas. These red pandas help them earn money through tourism which is used to fund the protection of the forest. Also, in the high areas of Arunachal Pradesh, the Panchen Red Panda Conservation Alliance has been formed to help protect a forest area of 200 square kilometers.

# Did You Know? - Fun Facts about the Red Panda

Learn more about the different fun details about the cute yet evasive red pandas:

The red pandas have lots of names, including: Petit Panda, Small Panda, Lesser Panda, Bear-cat, Bright Panda, Cat-bear, Firefox, and Poonya

Red pandas can grow and live to between 12 – 14 years.

Over the winter season, the red pandas often lose about 15% of their total body mass.

They clean their body parts the way cats do by licking.

They are shy animals

## Popular Red Panda Celebrities

The red panda has been an inspiration to a number of cartoon characters. Japan's red panda Futa, has inspired the character Bolin's animal companion named Pabu in the Nickelodeon cartoon series "The Legend of Korra". Also, Kung Fu Panda's Master Shifu, is based on red pandas. Shifu is the Kung Fu teacher of lead character, Po, and has been a part of the cartoon movie's continuing franchise. In the cartoon movie, "Barbie as the Island Princess", Sagi is a red panda who is a close friend to Barbie. Sagi has also been featured in a number of items of Barbie merchandise.

# Testing What You Have Learned:Comprehension Questions

Answer the following questions and see how much you have learned about red pandas:

1, How long does a mother red panda carry its babies in the womb before giving birth?

2. Give at least 5 from the many names given to red pandas.

3. Are red pandas carnivores, herbivores or omnivores?

4. What comprises about two thirds of a red panda's diet?

5. What is the name of Japan's famous red panda known to stand upright for about 10 seconds at a time?

6. What are the two subspecies of red pandas?

7. IUCN considers red pandas as _____ creatures because there are only an estimated 10,000 red pandas in the world.

8. The red pandas are members of the _____ family.

9. In early 1990s, the red panda was considered a mascot in Sikkim, India for what festival?

10. How many months does it take before a red panda becomes fully matured?

# Comprehension Answer

1. 112 to 158 days

2. Petit Panda, Small Panda, Lesser Panda, Bear-cat, Bright Panda, Cat-bear, Firefox, and Poonya

3. Omnivores

4. Bamboo

5. Futa

6. Styan's red panda and Western red pandas

7. Vulnerable

8. Musteloid

9. Darjeeling Tea Festival

10. 3 months

# More Pictures

Made in the
USA
Middletown, DE